i used to
be the sun

i used to
be the sun

Valeria Eden

Rev. date: 11/02/2018

To order additional copies of this book, contact:
Xlibris
1-888-795-4274
www.Xlibris.com
Orders@Xlibris.com
780429

this book exists because someone believed in me. someone who saw the light in me when i was convinced there was none to be found. thank you, my love. this is for you.

to whomever finds this book, please know that you are holding my heart in your hands. treat it gently. do the same with your own.

The Setting

i wish that i could think of you and remember all of the times we loved without question, the smiles we shared, swaying to lord huron in my kitchen, the way our souls embraced, or the days and nights that i started and ended by curling into your chest.

but whenever you cross my mind, every happy memory is tainted by the one where you left when i needed you to stay.

all i do is wholeheartedly

give myself to people

and somehow i am still surprised

when they take

instead of give back

forever

or until one of us loves less

some days

i wonder how the sun feels

and if she is tired of burning herself up

just to keep everyone else warm

i wonder

whether or not she knows

that she is killing herself to shed light

on a planet that is also dying

i think about whether or not she is lonely

if she too knows how it feels

to be isolated in a crowd

some days

i wonder

whether or not it is a compliment

when people tell me

that i remind them of sunshine

i have anger boiling in my bloodstream

and concentrated misery in my bone marrow

i was always destined to burn myself up from the inside out

maybe there are parts of ourselves that we will never stop hiding

i miss the feeling of shared skin. yours, and mine, and ours-brushing against the bareness of each other's shoulders as our chests leaped with laughter and until they ached from it.

after *The Day* in November, sometimes in class i would forget until i turned around that i wouldn't be met with your messy, sun-bleached hair and crooked grin, only "*i miss you's*" and "*i wish you were still here's*" littering your desk in neon colors that tried too hard to be the kind of bright that you were. "*gone too soon*" some of them said. as if the days surrounding your sudden absence were opaque blurs, as if the world didn't stop turning, as if breath wasn't hard to take in anymore, as if time hadn't slowed down enough to conjure every crease, and edge, and line of the smile that used to coax out mine. as if it were not a type of death in itself realizing that *now,* memory was all i had.

i don't remember what day your funeral was but i do know that it was the first time i hated the color red. in the soft waves of your coffin it was the first thing i saw. the crimson line curled proudly around your neck, like it belonged there. like it was a thing of great accomplishment to take kisses and warm breath and replace them with an angry red reminder of how warmth will never again find a home there.

i hope you forgive me for not knowing that my sadness wasn't the absence of your own. i'm not much for proving myself to a god who's never proved himself to me, but if you see him, beg him to forgive me too. wherever you are now, i hope you're laughing. i hope your skin is heating someone else's and that you're still bouncing when you walk. when you smile, i hope one side still rolls up farther than the other. i hope you're still following your own rules and spreading love with your entire being. and wherever you are now, i hope you know that the warmth you left behind will always have a home with me.

-a letter to the lost

too many parts of me are tainted by memories of wandering hands and the unforgiving touch of cold metal. it's a subtle kind of cruelty, how the only things i want to leave me are the only things that stay. for so many years, people have told me that i reminded them of something golden and i didn't know how else to prove them wrong aside from slicing myself open and saying

see? there's nothing special here.

but there has to be some place within my skin and bones that is untouched and holy and

i haven't found it yet, but i will love you there when i do.

someone asked me how i still loved you after all of this distance and all of this heartbreak and i replied

the same way you can still drive the route to your childhood home with your eyes closed even after years of not doing so

it was a night where we were far enough away

from the pollution and the people and the polluted people of the city

to see the constellations

the moon was reflected in your eyes

your eyes were reflected in mine

and it was then that i decided

you would never be anything less than beautiful

you kept your head in the clouds

traced the sky with your gaze

and told me that the big dipper was a cliché

but in a way that i knew it was still your favorite

then you folded your hand into mine

and i wanted to curl into the space

between that moment

and the one where you would let go

instead i settled for resting my head

beneath the three freckles on your left collarbone

and on top of your heart

your bones rattled against my ear

as you took a breath and said to me

the real stars are in my lungs

and i can't breathe right when i look at you

i closed my eyes

against the brightness of it all

as you drove us back to the city

I

i wish that i could exist

in a way that didn't feel forced

that i could socialize

react

feel

love

in a way that didn't make me seem

like a puppet with broken strings

i wish that my human form

didn't rely on drugs to function

the way it is supposed to or

that every time i let a fragment

of my struggle escape through words

people wouldn't always have that

same pitiful look

i'm so glad that isn't me

but above all i am so tired

so **bone-achingly** tired

of mimicking animation when being alive

should come naturally but

maybe if i continue to pretend long enough

some day

i will get it right

i want to embody the color yellow

but i am always burning blue

- maybe one day

it copies the rain

trickling into your life like blood from a wound

weaving in and out

over and under

in between familiarity

and sometimes it pours but

you never learned how to swim

depression has its own alphabet

most days its language is the hardest to unlearn

the media glorifies it in a way that everyone believes

they are fluent in it

but they speak broken sentences

parodies

they don't understand the phonetics

the syntax

not like i do

sometimes in the mirror

i ask the stranger staring back at me

why are you always so sad?

she tilts her head at me and says

i don't know

i don't know

i don't know when

but at some point the world got heavier and i stopped being strong enough to carry it

i should have told you that your light drowned out the absence of my own

i've been setting small fires since the day you told me you wanted to
work with them and one day soon i hope the smoke envelops me and
burns me to the ground so you'd finally look at me instead of through me

to answer your question

yes

there is a difference between loving someone

and being in love with them

the latter is:

me, or my eyes,

getting lost in the galleries of yours

me, or my clumsiness,

painting an accidental smile on your face and

me, realizing that i want to keep a paintbrush in my back pocket

every second

of every day

of forever

just to do it again

me, or our hands,

joined together so perfectly as if they

were missing puzzle pieces

me, or my heart,

and how it has always been more yours than mine

the former is:

you, or your gaze,

and how it never held mine long enough to memorize

my eye color or how it changes

you, or your laugh,

and how it always seemed to

effortlessly bubble up at my expense

you, or your hands,

and how they tended to pull away from my own

you, or your heart,

and how it has never belonged to me

so to answer your question

yes

there is a difference between loving someone

and being in love with them

but i wouldn't expect you to know

i hope you felt more love than you showed

the bruises under my eyes

still match the color of your heart

and i am trying to remember

that this doesn't mean we belong together

ⵔ

i was cleaning the attic yesterday when i found a box of our photo albums. we were happy then.

i came across a picture of us sitting in that stupid swing in your backyard, the one that was uneven on the right side, but your dad built it for your mom and i always thought that things could be perfect even when flawed. i guess that didn't apply to us.

i wonder if you'd recognize yourself in that picture. you were looking at me like i put the sun in the sky, the way you always did, back when you used to be bilingual in laughter and love; before you became fluent in profanities and heartbreak.

i burned the box.

ⵀ

after falling out of love with you

i realized why hurricanes were named after people

and sometimes i still miss you

but not the rain you brought

not the thunder of your voice

or the lightning of your words

on those days where we

hated more than we loved

i do not miss the earthquake of my hands

when i turned into myself and away from you

or the snowflakes that formed on my eyelashes

those nights when you made it feel like

winter in the middle of June

and i do not miss the clouds hanging over us when i realized that i was
in a long distance relationship even though there were nothing but a few
inches between us

my heart still reaches out for yours in the middle of the night

i've been without you for so long that my mind has gotten used to your absence but when i saw you last week i realized that my body will never forget

growing up

i was often told to follow my heart

on the nights where the moon sees more of me than her sister does

i still wonder

but which piece?

if he tears down the walls you built

slides his hands over and under

your skin without your permission

if he does not commit your constellations

of freckles

scars

birthmarks

to memory

then *this is not love*

if he steals your breath

and keeps taking things

that do not belong to him

it is not love

if he wraps you in his arms

intertwining your limbs

as if they were never meant to be separated

and you feel safe

remember

sometimes birds feel safe in their cages

but that *is not love*

i remember the first time

you looked at me with stars in your eyes

when you caressed my skin with kisses

and warm fingertips

trailing up to the center of me

you hummed to the pulse of my heartbeat

and told me

i want to stay here forever

later

when the snow melted

and everything was less magical

i remember the first time

you looked at me like my mother did

and told me

i don't want your broken parts anymore

do you remember love, love?

do you remember us on those nights

where our eyes resembled candle flames

flickering back and forth between the sunset and each other

not being able to decide which was more captivating

being near you in those moments

felt like being enclosed in a snow globe

a perfect glass world that was entirely our own

but as the days bled into weeks

and our love turned into apologies

eventually your backpack became heavier

while my chest cavity became emptier

did you take my heart with you?

did you lose your own?

you can leave a broken home but it will never leave you. it will show in your posture, the length of time you can maintain eye contact, the people you surround yourself with, how long you can hold a steady job, and whether or not you can sleep with your door unlocked. but hopefully, one day i can look at all of these things within myself and only see one thing:

freedom.

i think my hands were always dewed with sweat around you because they knew we should keep a layer between us.

it made things easier when you left.

i've been told by ex-lovers, in their final, desperate attempt to hurt me as i have hurt them,

*you **really** are your father's daughter*

you look so much like him

and you never learned how to to stay when people need you

why are you always leaving?

why are you always running?

i don't know how to tell them that staying feels like settling; it feels too comfortable. it feels like unpacking my baggage, unboxing my burdens, giving them a home to live in. a place to rest, someplace for *me* to rest

but i have been escaping since age ten, outrunning any chance of stability because the house i grew up in had none. there was no gravity.

at a young age, i learned that love can ground you. but the day my father left, my mother floated away and i have been drifting ever since. so then, i learned that love can also leave you.

so: yes. i am my father's daughter.

the most important lesson he ever taught me is that it is always better to be the one who leaves first.

i hope that your next lover tastes *my* love on your lips

and that she breathes in the ghost of me that lingers

in every tender part of you

i want her to know that i made a home out of you once

and even though i have moved out and you have moved on

my name will always be signed on your heart like a confession

the only relief i feel these days is when i am unconscious

i dream of waking up in a colorful world

a place where everything is not covered

by shades of gray or tainted by splintered memories

the sunset doesn't remind me of

holding hands with you beneath it

and the floorboards of my apartment

don't bear the forgotten weight

of us slow dancing in the kitchen

things are peaceful here

when i look in the mirror she smiles back at me

her eyes are full of life and her cheeks

full of warmth

i dream of a world

where our paths never crossed

we are still strangers

both looking for love

but never finding it in each other

and therefore never losing it

love doesn't live here anymore. it used to, in every bedroom. we used to have no windows, to let the light in. you liked it better that way, and i was secretly terrified of the dark. but the glow faded, as it tends to do, and during every sunset, you noticed that the warmth went with it. i started scalding myself in the shower, thinking that maybe this building didn't have to be a home to warmth if only i could learn how to be. i let my body turn pink and then boil into red, whispering apologies to my puckered skin that it would be worth it. but i couldn't be the sun for you, blue is the only color i've ever known how to be.

love doesn't live here anymore. it doesn't know how to.

grief is the embodiment of my family home

it's the foundation that it was built on

and though the walls are always changing color

layers of paint can't cover up something we will always know

anger is my sharp-tongued mother whose words cut like knives

and how people tell me i look more like her every day

loss is my father lying 6 feet underground

beneath a garden of flowers and the weight of heartache

strength is in my name

embedded in my bones

and even though my parents struggled to name me

it's fitting.

it had to be fitting; perfect. i had to be perfect.

somewhere between the brainstorming, google searches, and endless pages of baby books, they settled on *Valeria*. "to be strong."

20 years later, sometimes i wonder if the meaning died with my father, if my mother had to rename me on her own, and chose the first thing she saw when she looked at me through the lens of her sorrow: disappointment.

but then i remember that a name only defines you if you let it. my middle name means *delight* and that is with what i choose to look at the world, despite it all.

it hurts, you know. the absence of people who took parts of you with them, that burning sensation of losing pieces of yourself that you always told yourself you needed.

i wonder if i will ever feel whole again, if i will have to sleep on a twin mattress for the rest of my life just so there's not enough space for the bed to feel empty, or if i will ever be able to pass a mirror without wondering what about me made you want to stop looking.

i never believed in the paranormal until my past started haunting me

and i can't sleep much these days

my ghosts keep me awake

they tug at my heartstrings and pull on my vocal cords

constricting my throat until i have no room to breathe

there are *too many* ghosts in this house

too many empty smiles and broken promises

not enough light

not enough love

my hands still reach out for warmth

in the middle of the night like they forget

that is hasn't touched the inside of these walls in years

our living room is a graveyard

dusty photographs of better times with better people

take up space where they can and i hold my breath as i pass-

it's disrespectful to breathe around the dead and i know that

who i was in those pictures is not coming back

there are too many ghosts in this house

and i am starting to feel like one of them

❧

it's been months since i've recognized my own reflection

but i still wave to be polite

❧

your absence makes its presence known in almost everything

there are tan lines across my hips where your kisses should be
calluses against my fingertips in place of the memory of yours
even my house feels different
less lively
more haunted

my heartbeat gets erratic sometimes
i think it believes that if it could just go faster
maybe time will follow its lead
and you'll come back to us

there is a world map that rests inside the left drawer of my desk and
when i miss you i fold it up until your location and mine look only one
finger jump apart instead of miles and hours and days

i miss your voice even though it still plays in my head. i miss your hands, despite how long it's been since i have held them. nights where our hearts would pound to the same song are just memory now. but i hope this isn't sad, because it isn't supposed to be. i am so glad to have loved you, and felt it in return. i just miss you.

stranger

what kind of tea do you like?

sit down on the sofa

or follow me into the kitchen

make yourself comfortable

don't worry about taking your shoes off

i doubt you'll stay too long

lover

come back to bed

down the hallway we christened with our laughter

left at the corner where you professed your love

into my neck

over my collarbone

down my stomach

through the pale door to my room

which is also the door to yours

come embrace me as lovers do

because isn't that what we are

friend

you look so tired lately

let me sing you to sleep

with the memories we used to make

back when the sun shone

more than it didn't

stranger

here's some earl grey for the road

close the door gently behind you

leave your key under the welcome mat

tread lightly through the garden we grew

and don't look back

but please

don't forget

hearts are not houses

you cannot rent a new one if the original falls apart

fear feels like gripping your phone so tight that your knuckles become white in an attempt to get closer to the voice on the other end while screaming

i'm here i'm here i'm here

i am sitting inside my public library

surrounded by words and somehow i still struggle

to find my own. the right ones.

i try to grasp sentences from my head

dismantle them and redesign them

to form on my tongue

exit my lips

or spring from my hands.

i know what i want to say

but *how do i say it?*

there are so many different highways

of stories floating around inside of me

i am so full of combinations

of letters

and numbers

and languages

and somehow

they all feel wrong

-*social anxiety*

A

at what age did we stop living and assume the motion of it?

B

memory fades with age

this is the only reason you are told that time can heal

&

when you found me

i was covered in indigo

shades of blues and purples

intertwined themselves around my skin

so tightly that neither of us

knew where to begin unraveling

you told me a story to make the time pass

telling me how you discovered

that yellow was your favorite color

it took weeks to tell

every day there was a new reason

to stick around

it was because of that dress i wore on a tuesday

the sunrise we watched the next morning

the color of my hair during golden hour

by the end of your story

which i thought had become ours

the bruises dotting my skin had faded

the sharp edges

became smooth again

but i guess i was still a few shades too dark

of the right kind of yellow

or maybe you had picked a different color

to fall in love with

and i'm sorry

that i couldn't be the rainbow

sometimes i can't get past the rain

Death didn't come in threes

he came in-

he **took**

one, two, three, four, five, six, seven.

Death seems to come

for everyone around me

the people who deserve it least

the souls who still have so much to give

for some reason i am always untouched

Death seems uneasy around me

always making sure to never be closer than

a few feet

a few inches

a few seconds away

he hovers just on the edge of my peripheral

so near that i can call out and say

please, take me instead

Death pretends not to listen.

there are points in time where my hands feel too heavy. they can't lift themselves from my sides anymore and my eyelids fall with them. some days the world is too dark. i exist in between shades of gray-not the pretty kind. not the romanticized wisps of gray that dance from your lips after you exhale a cigarette, or the dark steel color of your bed sheets, but more of the color gray that you shut your eyes and turn away from when it takes up the entire sky. the kind of dull that makes you think:

is this all there is?

sometimes the best kind of love comes with an expiration date

is this how it starts?

sweaty hands and stolen kisses

shallow breaths and shining eyes

how does it end?

don't spoil it.

i have given fragments of myself to everyone that i have ever loved
and i do not know how much of me is left

perhaps this is a good thing
maybe these parts of me will live on forever inside of other people
and i will be remembered for so much more
than a broken girl
with a broken body

things that suck:

1. goodbyes that are unsaid but felt

2. when you're finally comfortable in bed after a long day but then you aggressively have to pee

3. math

4. the ending of a *star is born* (what the fuck *was* that)

5. the fact that i gave you every single piece of me and you walked away entirely whole while i forgot who i was

6. the fact that i forgive you

7. the fact that i still love you

8. M A T H

9. olives

10. you can't love someone back to life

11. dogs don't live forever

12. regret

13. i can't erase you from my memory. i want to.

14. peanut allergies. i'm so sorry for you guys.

15. math fucking sucks

I

you've been saying goodnight like goodbye and maybe that's why every sunrise feels like a good mourning

B

time never seemed to matter to me until i ran out of it with you

i

i transform with the seasons and it was never fair of me to ask you to change with me

B

i wonder how long after our first kiss does the countdown begin to our
last

𝓑

when i am gone from this world

do not bring flowers to where my body rests

leave your heartache at home

keep our memories in the pictures

write on my headstone

nothing else has to die here

this is less prose and more of an apology for all of the times i have gotten it wrong. for the times i have failed: as a friend, as a lover, as a daughter, as a sister, as a human. i have not always done right by those i care about, and please believe me when i tell you that i am trying to do better. to be better. i have spent so long feeling trapped inside of this body, enclosed in a flesh prison that i never had a say in. i've been dealt cards that i never knew how to play with, and i've ended up losing more than just myself. forgive me. for taking my pain out on those who never inflicted it upon me. for being so unable to lift myself up that i wasn't strong enough to help you do the same, so i only pulled you down with me. i have spent 20 years rooted in self-hatred and so much sorrow, but i promise it ends here. i want to enclose myself in so much self-love that it pours out of me and embraces everyone i have ever loved, and ever hurt. i want to spend the rest of my life blooming into a woman you are all proud of, and i will. i will.

to my skin, my bones, my heart:

I'm sorry I'm sorry I'm sorry I'm sorry I'm sorry I'm sorry I'm sorry I'm
sorry I'm sorry I'm sorry I'm sorry I'm sorry I'm sorry I'm sorry I'm sorry
I'm sorry I'm sorry I'm sorry I'm sorry I'm sorry I'm sorry I'm sorry I'm
sorry I'm sorry I'm sorry I'm sorry I'm sorry I'm sorry I'm sorry I'm sorry
I'm sorry I'm sorry I'm sorry I'm sorry I'm sorry I'm sorry I'm sorry I'm
sorry I'm sorry I'm sorry I'm sorry I'm sorry I'm sorry I'm sorry I'm sorry
I'm sorry I'm sorry I'm sorry I'm sorry I'm sorry I'm sorry I'm sorry I'm
sorry I'm sorry I'm sorry I'm sorry I'm sorry I'm sorry I'm sorry I'm sorry
I'm sorry I'm sorry I'm sorry I'm sorry I'm sorry I'm sorry I'm sorry I'm
sorry I'm sorry I'm sorry I'm sorry I'm sorry I'm sorry I'm sorry I'm sorry
I'm sorry I'm sorry I'm sorry I'm sorry I'm sorry I'm sorry I'm sorry I'm
sorry I'm sorry I'm sorry I'm sorry I'm sorry I'm sorry I'm sorry I'm sorry
I'm sorry I'm sorry I'm sorry I'm sorry I'm sorry I'm sorry I'm sorry I'm
sorry I'm sorry I'm sorry I'm sorry I'm sorry I'm sorry I'm sorry I'm sorry
I'm sorry I'm sorry I'm sorry I'm sorry I'm sorry I'm sorry I'm sorry I'm
sorry I'm sorry I'm sorry I'm sorry I'm sorry I'm sorry I'm sorry I'm sorry
I'm sorry I'm sorry I'm sorry I'm sorry I'm sorry I'm sorry I'm sorry I'm
sorry I'm sorry I'm sorry I'm sorry I'm sorry I'm sorry I'm sorry I'm sorry
I'm sorry I'm sorry I'm sorry I'm sorry I'm sorry I'm sorry I'm sorry I'm
sorry I'm sorry I'm sorry I'm sorry I'm sorry I'm sorry I'm sorry I'm sorry
I'm sorry I'm sorry I'm sorry I'm sorry I'm sorry I'm sorry I'm sorry I'm
sorry I'm sorry I'm sorry I'm sorry I'm sorry I'm sorry I'm sorry I'm sorry
I'm sorry I'm sorry I'm sorry I'm sorry I'm sorry I'm sorry I'm sorry I'm
sorry I'm sorry I'm sorry I'm sorry I'm sorry I'm sorry I'm sorry I'm sorry
I'm sorry I'm sorry I'm sorry I'm sorry I'm sorry I'm sorry I'm sorry I'm
sorry I'm sorry I'm sorry I'm sorry I'm sorry I'm sorry I'm sorry I'm sorry
I'm sorry I'm sorry I'm sorry I'm sorry I'm sorry I'm sorry I'm sorry I'm
sorry I'm sorry I'm sorry I'm sorry I'm sorry I'm sorry I'm sorry I'm sorry

I'm sorry I'm

perhaps we are meant

to fall apart

to break

to burn

like a phoenix, this is how we rise.

The Rising

you will not find love buried inside of your cracked veins. but if you stop digging, and heal, you will find hope. and hope is enough.

i hope you learn to put your weapons down and remember that there are more important wars to be fought outside of your own skin

this body is your only home and it deserves so much respect for still standing after all of your battles fought against it

the moon is ethereal

and so are you

on nights that are darker than most

please remember that you both can still shine

and one morning, her eyes held more galaxies than gravity

i write so that i don't bleed

ↄ

we are so lucky

so infinitely fortunate

to be able to experience this world

to feel each other's hands

the warmth of summer on our skin

the blades of grass between our toes

while the birds sing to each other above us

and the wind dances by to their melody

i am so blessed

to begin and end my days

inside of this skin

that is all mine

forever

thank you

for this breath

this body

this life

ℬ

take up as much space as your human form allows and let these limbs become the only home you need

i have spent so many years dreaming of Death and yet he only takes people close to me.

i have wasted so much time mourning the losses of my friends, my family, and the parts of myself they took with them-the parts i will never get back-that i have forgotten how lucky i am to be here. sometimes, i am still more lost than i am found. the cold air in my lungs might feel like needles, my chest feels like caving in on itself, and the thoughts in my mind whirl by so quickly that i feel like a visitor inside of my own head who is dizzy just from being alive. yet, i am alive, and i am so lucky to be able to feel these things.

Death still finds his way into my head, but i no longer want to let him in.

wander.

get lost.

rediscover yourself.

do it again.

i wish that i could tell you there was more to me than this.

more than my shaking hands, in constant withdrawal from the touch

of yours, more than the blue rivers of my veins that have been

cracked more times than i can remember,

more than my physical scars,

more than my mental ones,

more than my heartbeat that never learned the definition of steady.

i wish that i could say i am more than my stories,

that i was a director and not an actor in my own life.

that there is more to me than my parents and how they both left,

but in different ways. i want to tell you that i am more than my

mistakes-and i have made so many.

but i am also not less than my smile when it is genuine,

my eyes in direct sunlight and how they are proof of a fire burning

within me. i am not less than a being of light wrapped in skin still

searching for her place in the world.

i am a summation of all of my misery and all of my joy.

right now, that has to be enough.

✑

do you want to hear the truth?

the world will swallow your dreams and spit them back out until you

don't recognize them anymore. your parents might tell you they hate

you, and maybe they'll mean it. when your first lover says "forever"

it will be much shorter than you planned. people will carve pieces of

you away and leave the knife behind but

you will pull it out and you will heal.

you will learn to depend on your own calloused but reliable hands.

religion?

want to know what i've learned?

i don't know if there is a god or not but i can tell you that when i was

watching my mother screaming on the tile floor for my father to

come back and my little brother was shaking

in the corner of her room, there sure didn't feel like one.

friends?

you will go through so many it's amazing that you will even

remember their names. but you will remember everyone that has

come and has gone.

love?

it tore my family apart. perhaps maybe not love itself, but the

absence of it.

home?

i felt safer in his arms than i ever did in a building.

your house might feel like a prison or a safe haven but either way

i hope it never feels like mine.

do you want to hear the truth?

there will be days where you want to rip out your heart and the rest

of yourself right along with it. there will be days where you want to

give up. but there will also be days where you find God in the cracks

of the ground at 3 am on New Year's Eve, your next best friend will

hold your hair back and she will stay longer than the rest. your

mother will hug you and tell you that she is weak but she still loves

you and she is sorry. she doesn't hate you.

your lover will tell you "forever" and it will be longer than you

planned. these will be the moments you hold on to on the nights

where you want nothing more than to let go.

do you want to hear the truth?

you are going to get through this.

she turned her flaws into ammunition
wore her bruises like armor
made her scars look like tiger stripes

she walked with her arms wide open
and told the world
i am finally ready for you

hello, it's me again.

i'm still seeing the world in faded colors, but i've stopped searching for you in crowds. i'm no longer looking for pieces of you in people that i meet. shades of blue are just that; they don't take me back to your eyes anymore. the empty side of my bed is just more space for me to fill. i want my heart back. i am finally ready to bear its weight. this is my last voicemail. don't call me back.

sometimes i look over from the passenger seat

i breathe in the way your hair falls into your eyes

how you hum along to the radio

the position of your left hand on the steering wheel

and your right one folded into mine

in these moments it is clear to me

that even though we are still driving

i have already arrived at home

reminder:

there is never a wrong time or place to destroy your foundation and rebuild yourself from the ground up

i know that it can be hard
to believe in what you don't see
but please remember
that you cannot look at yourself the same way
others do
the way i do

you can't imagine the way breath catches in my chest
when you laugh-when your head tilts back
and a giggle dances its way up your neck
while your eyes shine brighter than any star

your existence is pure magic
if you can't believe that
at least believe me

you are a body made of stardust; the dying embers of a universe

and i think that is both beautiful and terrifying

outside my window

sunshine is melting away any trace of snowfall

the earth is taking herself back today

the flowers and the grass and the leaves

are waking up after their icy slumber

and climbing through the gaps in the sidewalk

the sky is blue today

almost as blue as his eyes that morning

when sunlight illuminated the way he looked at me

when we were both happy and awake and together

-spring

revel in it

sink into the embrace of love and burn the feeling

into the deepest parts of your memory so when it is gone

the light it brought will remain with you

when your demons drown out the sky tell them that they are wrong

say to them that you remember a better time and because of that

you will fight for a better future

scream out to their voices

you have been loved

you are loved

you can love

you will love

you deserve love

i could write a thousand poems about your heartbeat

about the calmness of it and the guideline it creates

for my own restless one

i could write stories about how our hands met

how it was like they were made for each other

how they fell in love and

how they could never separate after that

i could write fairytales about your eyes

the way they shine when you look at me

the colors they change into depending on your mood

and how whenever they close when kissing me

it's always followed by a smile

i could write songs about your voice

about the melody of it and how you make music

out of your words and hymns from your laughter

but i will start with writing

this

and reminding you each day

that every part of you

deserves to be written about

i want to spend each life by your side, crossing into the next one together, surrendering to love even when we are ghosts. let's haunt young couples and make them so afraid of the idea of ever being apart. let's terrify them with the thought of love lost, so that they never stop finding it in each other. let's show them what happens when they choose each other, over and over again.

it was six am on a sunday,

the sun had not woken up yet, but we had, in each other's arms. we battled sleep off our eyelids, pulled on clothes, and smiled the entire distance to my car. the air was warm and the sky was dark, but the inside of that car was filled with the brightest light i have ever seen. you are my own early morning, the dawning of a new day, the beginning of an adventure, a fresh start.

you move like a daydream. steady, but fluid, like you could fall through my fingers at any moment. you kept your eyes on the road while i kept my eyes on you, and our intertwined hands. we raced to the shoreline, trying to outrun the sunrise. the stars were disappearing, and the world was turning shades of pink, orange, and blue as you parked the car by the beach. we pressed our toes into the sand just as the sun was climbing out of the ocean and over the horizon, gently drifting up to take her place among the clouds. she radiated warmth onto our skin, and we reveled in it, dancing together in the sea foam, finding comfort in our laughter twisting together. i let go of your hand to capture our smiles in a picture, but the lens will never do your eyes justice. they reflected the color of the waves, and in that moment, i wanted to drown in them. you chased me back onto the sand, caught me in your arms, and pressed your lips into mine. my soul felt at home next to yours, and when we collapsed onto the blanket beneath us, i thought

i want to remember this forever.

we rolled onto our bellies and turned our faces away from the sun and toward each other. you rested your cheekbones on the back of your hand, and i got lost in your eyes again. the kaleidoscope of greens, and blues, with a hint of hazel became my favorite form of art. i closed my own eyes and fell into the feel of you, into the sound of the ocean, the birds, and the breeze. when it was time to leave, i didn't mind much-because wherever we are, if it's together, i am right where i need to be.

it is so important to sit with your darkness.

embrace it, become familiar with its edges. hold it in your hand, and be gentle with it. offer it comfort, offer it a place to rest. you don't have to shed light on the dark parts of you, it exists where it needs to. it will not stay forever.

icy fingers wrap around your heart, threatening to steal its warmth.

you remind yourself of everything that it beats for:

the feel of raindrops on your skin

the sound of his voice in the morning

two am kisses and two pm laughs

the taste of strawberries against your lips

and the color that they leave behind

car rides with songs that pull words from you

that you had thought were forgotten

happy reunions and drawn out goodbyes

your heart pumps life throughout your body,

keeping you alive for all of the moments you have yet to discover.

the ice melts inside your rib cage, for it has never felt warmth like

yours before.

-a dream

yesterday i felt the sun on my skin again and i thought

this is the meaning of life, these moments that make you appreciate it

maybe this is what love really is

it's not whether you've loved and lost, or never loved at all-
maybe it's simply meeting someone worth missing

ᢒ

most days are beautiful

some are not

but on *those* days

i will measure the things worth living for in the way that your eyes

personify light when you talk about what you love

in the way that your hand steadies my anxious one

and is always equally as sweaty

and in the number of breaths we take to smile before kissing again

i will measure them in the moments where Time closes her eyes

and just lets us be

lets us pull into each other until there is no more space between

your skin and mine and i can feel the tempo of your heartbeat

-always slower and steadier than my own-

Time can't touch us here

in the nights when everything is just dark enough

that i am able to lookup toward the constellations and realize

that we are so incredibly small

but so are the stars

and neither of us will ever be insignificant

in how sometimes i will find a song that somehow perfectly matches

the flow of blood in my veins

and

even though my thoughts are as fleeting and unstable as a

hummingbird

some days

i am so irrevocably and utterly in love with this life

and all it has to offer that i remember *this*

all of this

makes today beautiful too

once

so long ago it feels like a dream more than a memory

you asked me what love felt like

i answered back

when love finds you, you'll know

i never expected to rediscover its meaning alongside you

but now if you ever forget what love feels like

i'll remind you over and over again

repeat after me:

i am a *fucking* warrior and i will never forget it again

ℬ

brokenness is not a fixed state of being

it implies that there is room for repair

and this means that there is hope for you

love is when he holds your heart with both hands until you are ready to bear its weight again

when they don't love you in return

the willow trees add another year of weeping onto their lives

but when you do not love yourself

that is a heartbreak so colossal there are tsunamis on every coast

we were sitting on the edge of the river, legs intertwined

she tucked a strand of hair off my cheek and said

god, your smile is vibrant. you are the sun.

i looked up at her through my eyelashes, could feel my face turning hot as i replied

no, but i used to be.

she took my hand in her own and told me

darling, you still shine bright enough for me.

<decorative flourish>

there are so many reasons

to turn certain humans away

from your companies

your restaurants

your homes

but for simply being human

should not be one of them

we are all born with skin and bones

why should we not be free to decorate them

however

whenever

we wish

the stories told in ink

encircling my arms

across my shoulders

should not affect you

they simply exist

as do you and i

the metal resting inside my cartilage

does not play a role in my intelligence

or ability to work

the way we adorn our human vessels

with jewelry

tattoos

clothing

makeup

hair color

none of these

not a single one

defines any of us

aside from those who judge

because of it

B

Time.

she is a fleeting thing
unstable and bound to no one

she takes or she gives or she freezes at random
but i still love her
for the moments she gives me
to exist unapologetically

i love her
when she stands still
and looks away
lets me kiss him
slow and warm and comfortable

i love her
because she is a teacher
some days she is forgiving
others she is not
but she teaches
and i learn

do not make yourself fold into spaces that you were always meant to outgrow

dance with who you currently are on sunday mornings and take a break from the pictures that beg you to remember the past because who you are now is who you are supposed to be *now*

ᘒ

i wish that all of our demons were nameless but maybe we can baptize them in our love and show them that the labels we were given are not the ones we have to keep

ᔕ

bloom through your pain. create magic from your heartache, and watch
how beautiful it becomes.

long ago, there lived two sisters: Love and Loss. they were the daughters
of Joy and Grief. Love was named after the beginning of her parents'
relationship, and Loss, after the ending of it. they lived in one of those
buildings that rested on the line between being a house and being a
home, in one of those neighborhoods where everyone knew each other,
but didn't want to. the sisters were polar opposites. Loss was often
compared to snow. she was beautiful, but cold. she often kept to herself,
reading books about broken things and broken people. Love was warm.
she personified sunshine in every way, with golden hair and freckles like
her mother; her father could never look her in the eye. but they were best
friends. Love was the only person her sister allowed to touch her. she
kept everyone else at arm's length, in fear of her namesake. but Love was
different. Love understood Loss. after all, one could not exist without
the other.

one day, a boy moved in next door. his mother was one of those neighbors
that made herself known; baking cupcakes and pies of all kinds to pass
out so that people would remember her. of course, she dragged her
son along, wanting him to make friends (he was never good at that.)
people often cast him aside for someone more than him. more fun,
more impulsive, more easygoing. so on the day that his mother was too
busy baking to come knock on their neighbors' door with him, he was
not expecting to make a friend. neither was Loss. she never answers
the door when she's home alone, choosing to avoid conversation when
unnecessary. so she didn't quite understand what pulled her to the door
that day, and away from her book. she didn't know why she engaged in
more talking than she usually does, nonetheless with a stranger, but
when she closed the door, there were three things in her possession
that Loss did not have when she opened it. a smile, a blueberry pie, and a
name. "They call me Forgiveness," he had told her.

forgiveness will give you wings,

hatred will give you anchors.

fall in love with your reflection, because that will become your greatest love story.

look in the mirror and repeat after me:

i love you. every inch of your skin that is marked with stories of how far you've come. the shape of your eyes that have seen so much. i love your lungs, they allow you to breathe here with me. i love your limbs and how they work just the way they were meant to. your smile is dazzling. you shine so bright, always, in all ways. i love your capacity to love. your heart is so beautiful. you are so beautiful. i am beautiful. i am, i am, i am.

❧

love is how you changed its definition

it's no longer something out of reach

something i search for on bookshelves

it's in the way you look at me

as if you finally found me after years of being lost

it's in the feel of your lips when pressed against mine

warm and familiar and dizzying

it's the ebb and flow of pressure between our joined hands

how they remind me of the sea kissing the shoreline

sometimes they are apart but never for too long

i miss you when we are apart

the way you embody joy with every breath

how your eyes change color like the seasons and

how they made me want to take up art

i hope you are always like the ocean

headstrong and unpredictable

mesmerizing and unapologetically yourself

always returning back home-

i hope whenever someone tells you to go home

you find your way back to me

B

instead of being consumed by the ways life has wronged me i will
celebrate the events that have made me stronger and reminded me to
be gentle

B

i'll love you within your darkness as long as you stay when i find my light

i feel illuminated today

snow is falling outside my window

the world is lazy and gentle and painted white

and for once i want to take up space

the snowflakes are planting kisses on the earth

as if reuniting with her for the first time

in a long time

and it is cold and it is beautiful

and i have been envious of this for so long

that i have forgotten there is also beauty in being warm

there is bravery in being vulnerable

the pavement has an iridescent blanket over it

if not for the faint voices drifting by

i would almost believe that the world was asleep

but she is not and i am not

and there is beauty to be found in that too

-stream of consciousness

whenever

wherever

however

this ends,

i will lock the memory of us in a room inside my heart for safekeeping.
in case we ever want to revisit it, i will hide the keys to our door in the
empty spaces between our fingers, underneath the dip in your collarbone
where i planted kisses to bloom when you are sad, and on top of the
curve of my waist where you rested your hand after pulling me into you.

if any of these are ever lost, i'll place the doorbell on top of our lips,
where it will only ring if they meet again. our old smiles, laughter, and love
will answer the door, and welcome us home.

love people while they are still here

on days where everything is on fire and it burns too brightly i hope you realize that you are your own sun and no one can take that from you

i want to give you the world, maybe not really the whole world, just the good parts. for daffodils and daisies to bloom between the spaces of your ribcage so that when everything seems dark you will still know that there are parts of you that are divine.

i want snowflakes to kiss the backs of your hands and melt into your bloodstream to remind you to appreciate the small things.

i want the tides to pull our moon closer to your window so when you feel lonely, you can look up at the sky and remember that you are not.

this might all be gone by morning,

but isn't it a beautiful night?

the city moves too fast sometimes and my heart beats too slow but when our hands meet everything feels peaceful and still

don't forget to fall in love with more than just people but if you insist on loving human souls then please know it is okay to put your own first

picture this:

you wake up. early.

in sync with the sun and the birds that follow.

you wake up in a hazy hue of colors that slowly fade into a constant.

you wake up.

not because your mother pulled the blinds open

or because it was time to be a functioning human again

you wake up because you want to be alive

and *it is quiet.*

the voices in your head have nothing to say.

you lazily swing your brightly colored toes over

the edge of your sanctuary and step in front of the mirror.

for once, the only thing you see staring back at you is a smile

that has finally found its home.

-recovery

love.

until it runs out.

until it fades away.

until it finds someone new.

and then

love again.

love anyway.

thank you.

Made in United States
North Haven, CT
10 November 2021